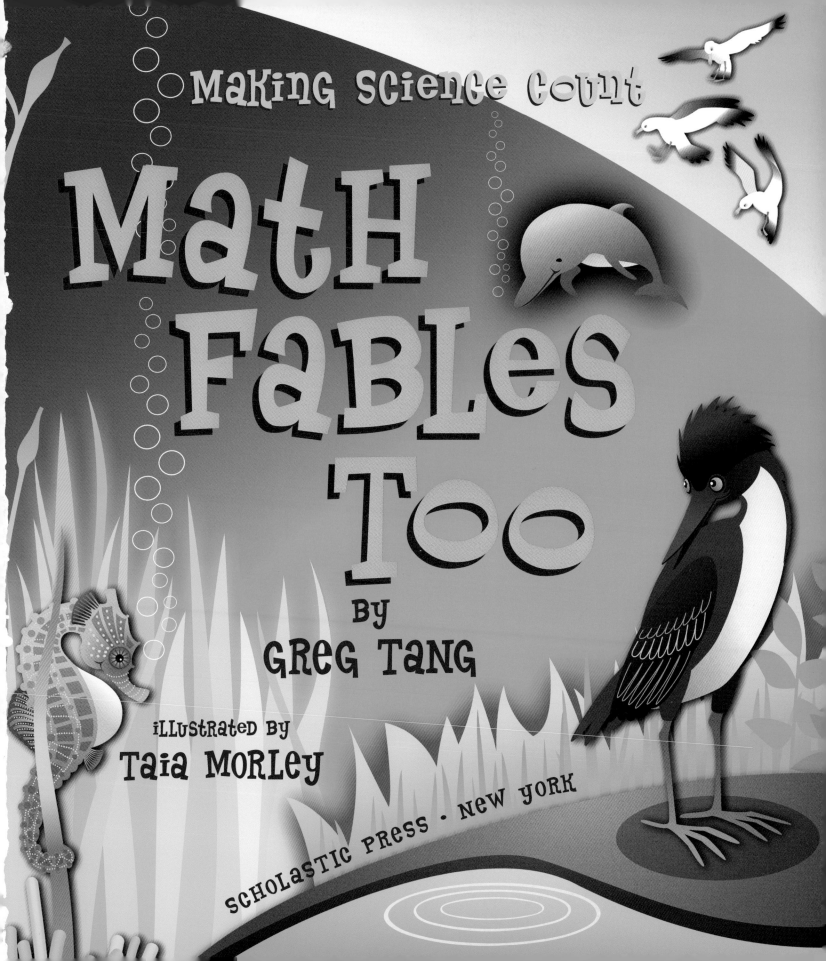

Making Science Count

Math Fables Too

By
Greg Tang

Illustrated by
Taia Morley

SCHOLASTIC PRESS · NEW YORK

With Love to Katie

G.T.

For Kathy Berrigan,
a gracious and lovely teacher of math

T.M.

Library of Congress Cataloging-in-Publication Data

Tang, Greg. Math fables too : making science count / by Greg Tang ; illustrated by Taia Morley.

— 1st ed.   p. cm.

1. Counting — Juvenile literature. 2. Science — Juvenile literature. I. Title.

QA113.T3555 2007   513.2'11 — dc22   2006028970

ISBN-13: 978-0-439-78351-4   ISBN-10: 0-439-78351-8

10 9 8 7 6 5 4 3 2 1   07 08 09 10 11

Printed in Singapore 46 • First edition, September 2007

The display type was set in Stovetop.

The text type was set in Myriad Condensed.

author's Note

every child's journey in math begins with counting. But it is the next step that is the most important of all: the transition from counting — or thinking one at a time — to adding, which requires thinking in larger, more efficient groups. Unfortunately, many kids never make this critical transition and secretly count their whole lives. No wonder they find math difficult!

My goal in writing this book is to help kids learn to count, and more importantly, to lay the groundwork for addition. From the time children are first exposed to numbers, I believe the secret is to encourage them to see numbers in terms of other numbers. When kids learn to decompose single-digit numbers at an early age, everything else — place value, arithmetic, problem-solving — follows naturally.

In each fable, I begin by introducing numbers as a single, countable group. As the stories unfold, I break the numbers into smaller groupings. The idea is to shift the emphasis from counting to adding, and from concrete to abstract thinking. I believe that making this shift at an early age is critical. Later, it is the kids who are comfortable thinking abstractly who do well in math.

In writing this book, I have several non-math objectives as well. First, I hope to encourage kids to become more interested in science by building on their natural fascination with animals. Each fable offers interesting, factual information together with clever problem-solving strategies. I am particularly interested in the use of tools by animals — behavior once thought unique to humans. Second, I intentionally use words that are difficult for my target audience, 3- to 7-year olds. I believe this is an ideal age to teach vocabulary since kids often read the same book many times.

Finally, I hope *Math Fables Too*, like *Math Fables*, offers kids positive messages that will benefit them in life as well as in school. The ultimate goal of all my books — *The Grapes of Math, Math for All Seasons, The Best of Times, Math Appeal, Math-terpieces,* and *Math Potatoes* — is happy, hardworking, smart kids who think creatively, independently, and love to learn. Enjoy!

Greg Tang

www.gregtang.com

SPECIAL DELIVERY

Among the blades of ocean grass,
1 sea horse swims alone.
His pouch is full of babies that
he's proud to call his own.

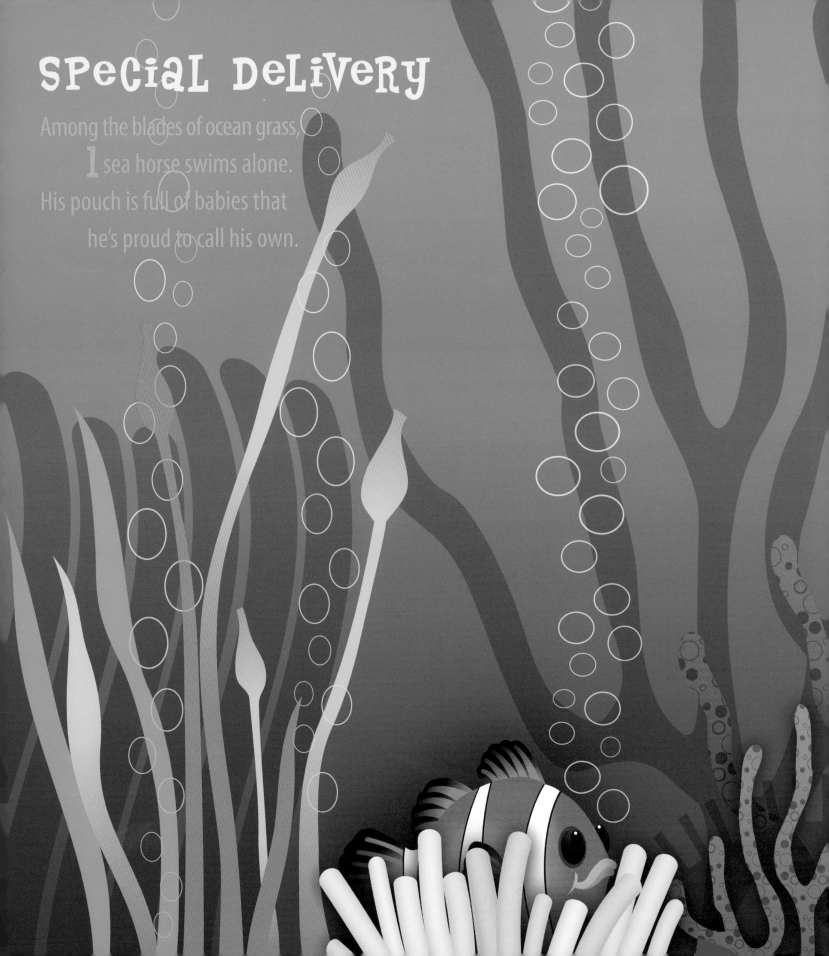

This pregnant dad's in fact a fish
blessed with a rare physique.
He's happy to be different—
it makes him more unique!

DAYDREAMS

One evening **2** koalas were
in search of something sweet.
They climbed a eucalyptus tree
with nimble hands and feet.

*This tree is very poisonous
to all but just a few.
Koalas are immune and so
the leaves are safe to chew.*

1 took a little nibble and
the other **1** a bite.
For these very picky eaters,
the leaves must be just right.

The **2** marsupials loved the taste
and ate the night away.
And since they are nocturnal—
they planned to sleep all day!

Nose Job

3 dolphins started foraging
along the ocean floor.
But stonefish hiding in the sand
soon made their noses sore.

These fish have quite a painful sting
and dolphins must beware.
The problem is they're camouflaged
and blend in everywhere.

2 watched as 1 smart female placed
a sponge upon her snout.
Her nose was now protected as
she rooted all about.

This very clever method was
adopted by all 3.
They say that imitation's the
best form of flattery!

FeatHeR Wait

One warm and breezy summer day
down by the marshy shore,
a group of herons gathered there,
a feathered flock of **4**.

Green herons are a cunning bunch
and lure the fish with bait.
Instead of chasing after them,
they lay a trap and wait.

3 herons used a feather and
another **1** a twig.
The fish thought they were insects,
a pretty clever gig.

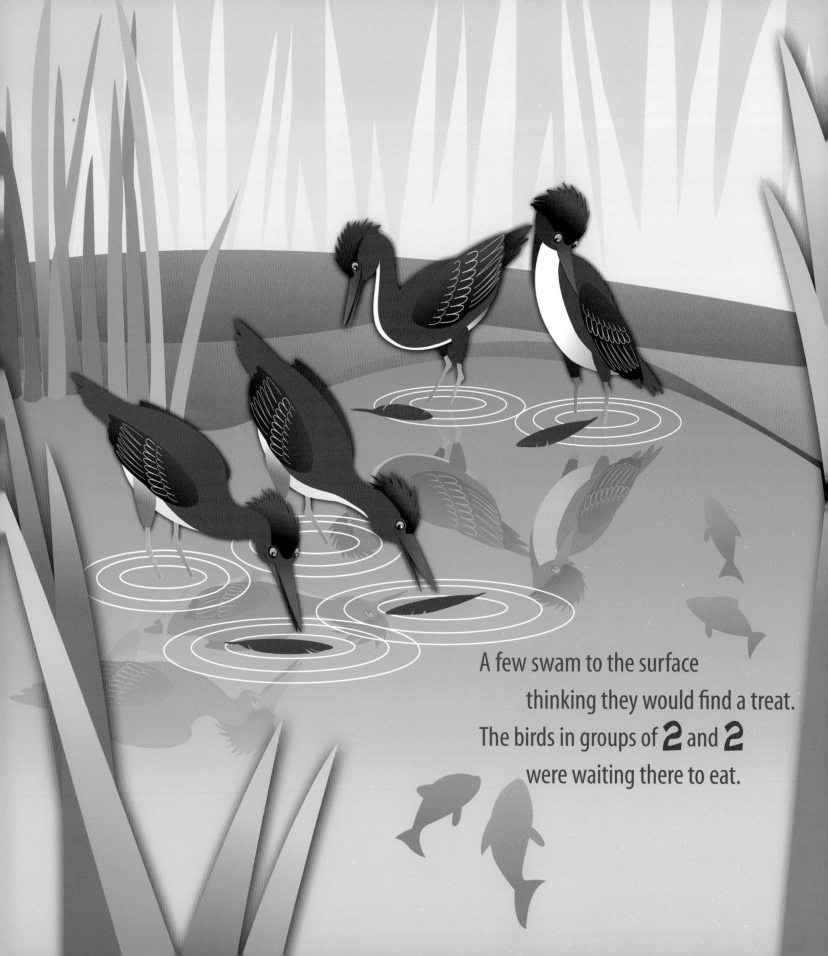

A few swam to the surface
thinking they would find a treat.
The birds in groups of **2** and **2**
were waiting there to eat.

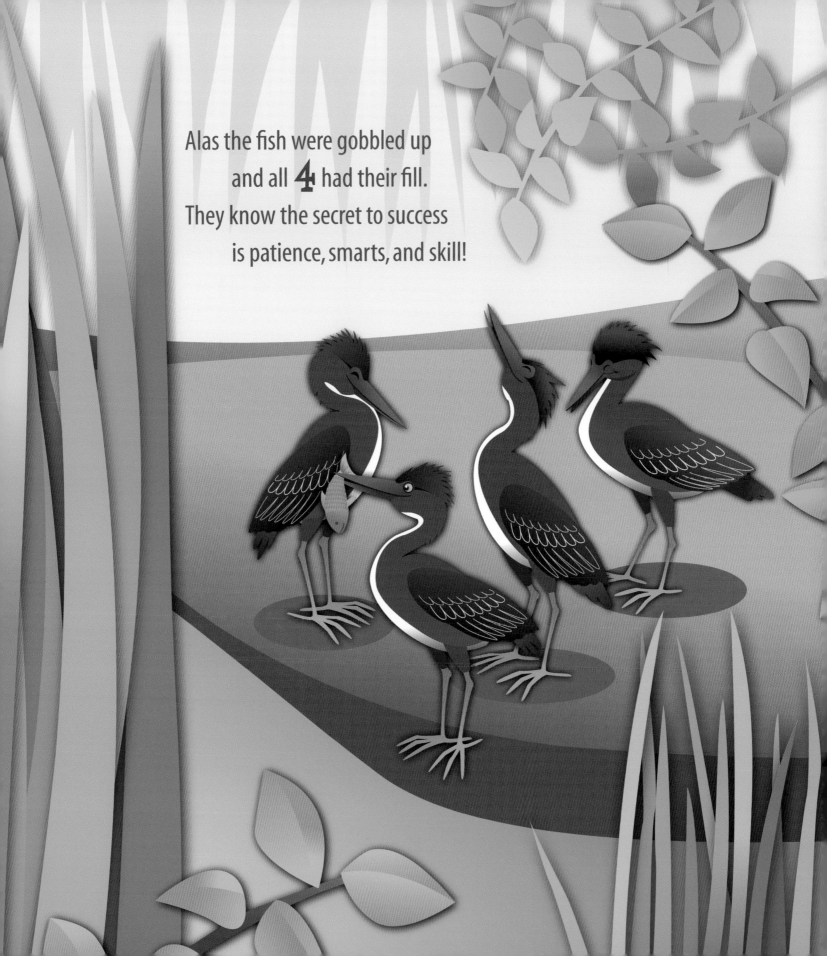

Alas the fish were gobbled up
and all **4** had their fill.
They know the secret to success
is patience, smarts, and skill!

COPiLotS

Inside a shallow ocean bay
5 pilot whales appeared.
Away from deeper water they
mistakenly had veered.

For whales it can be dangerous
to swim too close to land.
A tide that goes out rapidly
can beach them on the sand.

The youngest 1 swam to the front
and led the other 4.
They searched for open water but
were hemmed in by the shore.

The oldest whale swam up to help
and **2** now led the **3**.
They soon reversed direction and
swam safely out to sea.

Thanks to this very wise old whale
the pod had found its way.
All **5** of them safe home that night
knew wisdom saved the day!

KNOW SPITTING

Below the water's surface
6 fish waited patiently.
They knew that if their aim was good
they'd soon have company.

These fish have such a sneaky way
of catching what they eat.
They spit a stream of water that
knocks insects off their feet!

5 spotted several dragonflies
relaxing in the sun.
A brightly colored butterfly
was targeted by 1.

The archerfish then suddenly
in groups of 3 and 3,
spat water at the startled bugs
before they all could flee.

The insects lost their balance and
they landed with a SPLASH!
In groups of 4 and 2 the fish
then ate them in a flash.

All 6 were feeling quite content
with food enough for each.
They know that aiming high in life
leaves nothing out of reach!

THE SOUND
AND THE FURRY

The sun had set behind the hills
and dusk was on its way.
For **7** bats the time was right
to go in search of prey.

A bat can fly and hunt at night
by making little sounds.
The echoes locate insects that
are flying all around.

1 bat flew off into the sky
to hear what he could find.
6 others followed after him,
a flap or two behind.

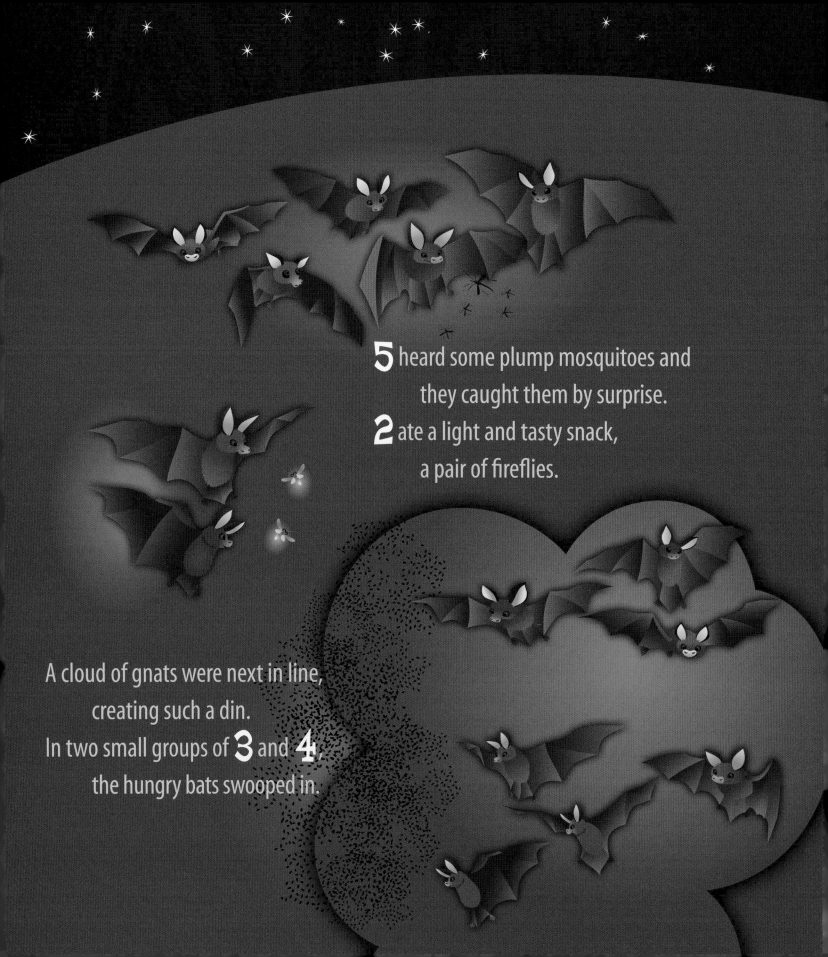

5 heard some plump mosquitoes and they caught them by surprise.
2 ate a light and tasty snack, a pair of fireflies.

A cloud of gnats were next in line, creating such a din.
In two small groups of **3** and **4**, the hungry bats swooped in.

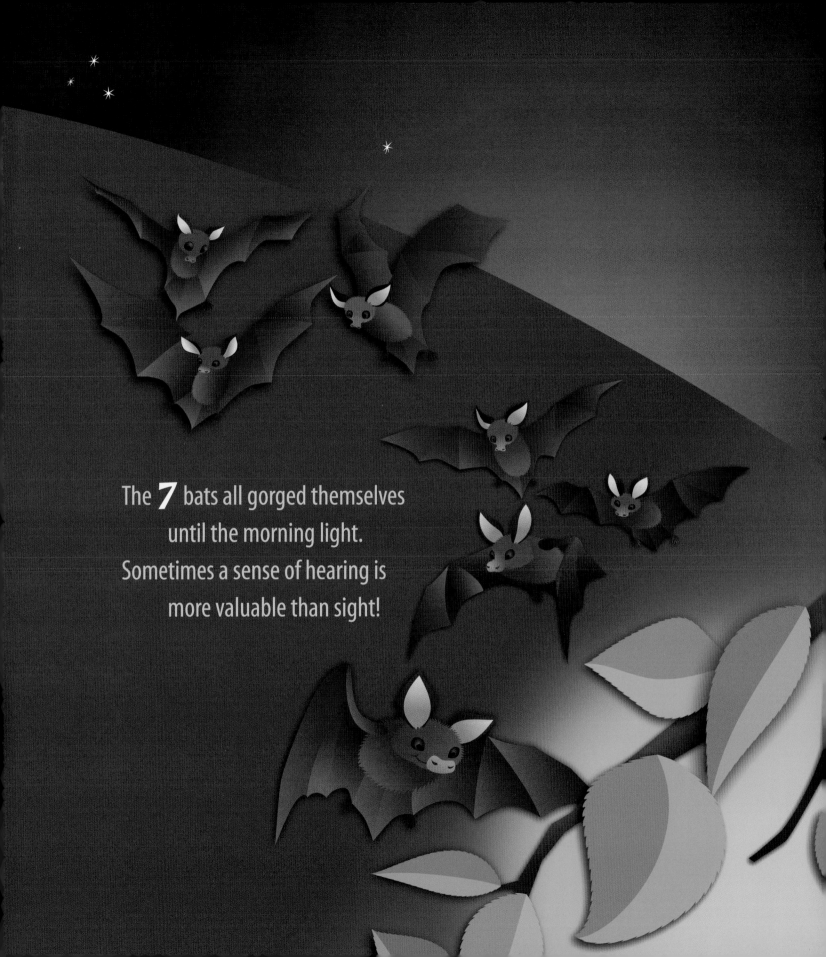

The **7** bats all gorged themselves
until the morning light.
Sometimes a sense of hearing is
more valuable than sight!

stones THROW

8 vultures circled overhead
   in search of scraps to eat.
When suddenly they spied below
   a most delicious treat.

In equal groups of 4 and 4
   they swooped down to the ground.
A nest of tasty ostrich eggs
   these scavengers had found.

The way they open up the shells
has made these birds well known.
Instead of using just their beaks,
they also use a stone.

In groups of 5 and 3 the vultures
pushed the eggs apart.
They had a plan for eating them
that proved to be quite smart.

1 picked a stone up in its beak
and carefully took aim.
The other **7** followed suit
and quickly did the same.

Then one by one they threw the stones
with **6** birds missing wide.
The other **2** both cracked the shells
and pecked their way inside!

All **8** would have a feast that day,
including those who missed.
Egyptian vultures know success
will come if you persist!

GO FISH

A forest in West Africa
9 chimpanzees call home.
For now it's safe from humans and
the apes are free to roam.

One day the chimps were playing when
1 saw a giant mound.
The other 8 looked closer and
found termites in the ground!

Now chimpanzees are much too shrewd
to dig into a nest.
They know when catching termites,
a simple tool works best.

2 showed the other 7
how to make a fishing pole.
They stripped the leaves from branches and
each poked one down a hole.

The chimps all waited patiently
in groups of 3 and 6.
And every now and then they checked
for termites on their sticks.

One termite here, two termites there,
a few found three or more.
The chimps enjoyed a healthy snack
in groups of 5 and 4.

All 9 spent that November day
just fishing in the sun.
They know that being clever is
the key to having fun!

SHELL GAME

The sun was shining brightly and
the winds were fairly light.
For **10** very patient seagulls,
at last the time was right.

All morning they had waited for
the tide to reach its low.
In equal groups of **5** and **5**,
now fishing they would go.

1 seagull caught a weary crab
who tried in vain to fight.
9 spied a tasty school of fish
and ate them in one bite!

The seagulls still were hungry when
2 birds let out a shout.
The other **8** rushed over and
found oysters all about!

While oyster shells are hard to crack,
  these birds are really smart.
They use the force of gravity
  to break the shells apart.

Each seagull grabbed an oyster and
  flew high into the sky.
And then in groups of **6** and **4**
  they let the mollusks fly.

3 found the broken oyster shells
and signaled to the rest.
The 7 hurried over and
they had an oyster-fest!

The 10 birds ate all afternoon
and left no shell unturned.
Smart thinking and persistence are
two lessons they have learned!

Sea horses are the only species in which the male becomes pregnant and gives birth. They are also unique among fish in having a prehensile, monkeylike tail that allows them to grab hold of plants for stability and each other during courtship.

There are over 300 kinds of eucalyptus trees, but koalas will eat the leaves of only about 3 dozen. Since these leaves are not very nutritious, koalas conserve energy by moving slowly and sleeping up to 20 hours a day.

Bottlenose dolphins near Australia are the first marine mammals known to use tools. Their creative use of cone-shaped sponges is a learned behavior that has been traced through DNA analysis to a single female dolphin — the originator of this technique.

Bait-fishing is neither innate nor culturally acquired. It happens rather by accident when herons inadvertently drop objects in the water. If they notice it attracts fish to the surface, some begin to intentionally drop objects as bait.

It is still a mystery why whales get stranded on beaches. They may become confused and swim too close to shore as a result of changing magnetic fields or odd coastal formations, or they may be simply following a sick or confused leader.

Archerfish can shoot water up to 10 feet in the air. To improve their accuracy, they've learned to overcome refraction — the bending of light as it passes from air to water — by spitting from directly beneath their target. They are also known to leap a foot out of water to snatch falling prey.

Bats use echolocation to navigate and catch prey at night. By emitting high-pitched sounds and listening for the echoes that bounce back, bats can identify the size and location of objects in their path. Toothed whales, which include dolphins, and some cave-dwelling birds also use this technique.

Egyptian vultures often have to throw a stone many times to crack an ostrich egg, despite the fact that the eggs are the largest in the world and can weigh up to 5 pounds. The vultures' aim is not very good, and these shells are very strong. They can support the weight of a 200-pound person.

Jane Goodall was the first person to observe chimpanzees fishing in the ground for termites. Chimpanzees also drink water by using partially chewed leaves to sop water up like a sponge, another example of their ability to make and use tools.

Seagulls are so smart they'll drop shells on parking lots instead of roads in order to avoid moving traffic. Their other favorite targets include hard-packed sand, large rocks, and rooftops of houses.